God Bless My Friend

God Bless My Friend

Illustrated by Betty Fraser

HALLMARK EDITIONS

Editorial Research: Beverly Simmons Bearly.
Editorial Direction: Aileene Herrbach Neighbors.

The publisher wishes to thank those who have given their kind permission to reprint material included in this book. Every effort has been made to give proper acknowledgments. Any omissions or errors are deeply regretted, and the publisher, upon notification, will be pleased to make necessary corrections in subsequent editions.

ACKNOWLEDGMENTS: "Friends Are Not a One-Way Street" by Marjorie Holmes from *Love and Laughter*. Copyright © 1967 by Doubleday & Company, Inc. Reprinted by permission. "Solaces of Life" by Thomas Curtis Clarke from "Fundamentals." Reprinted by permission. "Thank You, Friend" in *Poems of Inspiration and Courage* (1965) by Grace Noll Crowell. Copyright 1946 by Harper & Row, Publishers, Inc. Reprinted by permission of the publisher. "A 'Glad' Friend" from the book *A Thread of Blue Denim* by Patricia Penton Leimbach. © 1974 by Patricia Penton Leimbach. Published by Prentice-Hall, Inc., Englewood Cliffs, New Jersey. Reprinted by permission. "Borrowing" by John W. McKelvey and excerpt by Miguel de Unamuno from *The Treasure Chest*. © 1965 by Charles L. Wallis. Reprinted by permission. "The Art of Friendship" from *The Art of Living* by Wilferd A. Peterson. Copyright © 1960, 1961 by Wilferd A. Peterson. Reprinted by permission of Simon & Schuster, Inc. "Worthy of My Friends" from *Aim for a Star* by Helen Lowrie Marshall. Copyright © 1964 by Helen Lowrie Marshall. Reprinted by permission. "Beloved Memories" from *The Open Door* by Helen Keller. Copyright © 1957 by Helen Keller. Reprinted by permission of Doubleday & Company, Inc. "Down Life's Highway" by Emily Carey Alleman. Copyright 1957 by Emily Carey Alleman. Reprinted by permission. "Picture Puzzle" by Anne Campbell. Reprinted by permission. "Fireside Hour" by Katherine Edelman. Copyright 1954 by Katherine Edelman. Reprinted by permission. "Song for Back Doors" by Gladys McKee from the February 1942 issue of *St. Anthony Messenger*. Reprinted by permission. John 15:14-16 from the *King James Version Bible*. Reprinted by permission of the Cambridge University Press. Published by the Syndics of Cambridge University Press. "The Parable of the Good Samaritan" from the Gospel of Luke from the *Good News Bible* - Old Testament: Copyright © American Bible Society 1976; New Testament: Copyright © American Bible Society 1966, 1971, 1976. Used by permission of the American Bible Society and William Collins Sons & Company, Ltd.

© 1977, Hallmark Cards, Inc., Kansas City, Missouri.
Printed in the United States of America. Standard Book Number: 87529-528-2.

Friendship is the sun breaking through a cloud.
It is the fragrance of a flower
when a bud bursts into bloom.
It is the twinkling of myriad stars in the night sky.
It is the voice of God in the heart!

Thank God for My Friends

I think it is appropriate that the great old hymn "What a Friend We Have in Jesus" so elevates the earthly bond of friendship. For in our friends we find the truth, the strength and the unwavering faith that are very close to the Kingdom of Heaven. Thank God for my friends. They have stood by me through the years, sharing both my joy and my sorrow, enriching my life, reaching out to me wherever I might be. And thank God my friends in Christ will be with me always as we travel beyond this life into Life Everlasting. Friends are like the hands of God reaching out to us here on earth — strong hands that clasp our own and draw us ever closer to our Father in Heaven.

Billy Graham

I count this thing
to be grandly true:
That a noble deed
is a step toward God.

Josiah Gilbert Holland

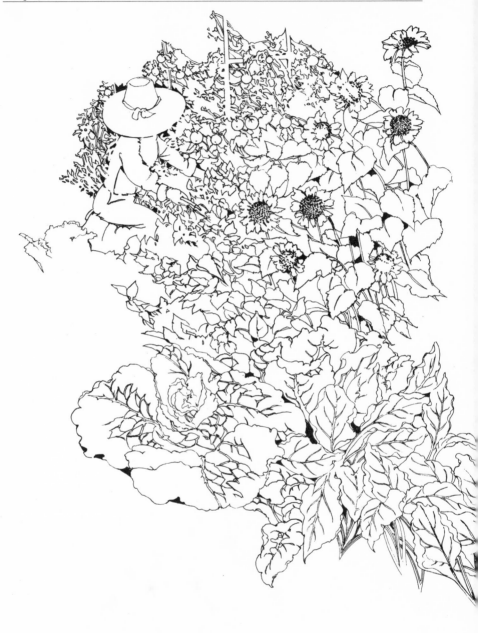

Summer Gifts

All spring I watched her in the sun,
Staking, hoeing, watering each one
With tender, loving care; now it was summer,
And I gazed out my window, a newcomer
To the neighborhood. First thing I knew,
My next-door gardener called to me: "Yoo-hoo!
I want to give you these, they're fresh and red —
A few tomatoes — and I've baked some bread!"

As I accepted the fruits of her labor,
I was gifted, too, with a new friend-neighbor!

Katherine Nelson Davis

If...

If you have a sense of humor
that makes things so much fun,
If you always have a friendly word
to say to everyone,
If you have a cheerful outlook
even when things may go wrong,
If you always have the time
to try and help someone along,
If you have a way of thinking up
nice favors you can do...
You're sure to have so many
who just think the world of you.

Karen Ravn

I cannot contentedly frame a prayer for myself in particular,
without a catalogue for my friends; nor request a happiness,
wherein my sociable disposition doth not desire the fellow-
ship of my neighbor.

Sir Thomas Browne

The Human Touch

An opal lay in the case, cold and lusterless. It was held a few moments in a warm hand, when it gleamed and glowed with all the beauty of the rainbow. All about us are human lives which seem cold and unbeautiful, without spirit or warmth, without radiance or gleam of indwelling light. Perhaps they need only the touch of a warm human hand, the assurance of love, to bring out the brightness of the spiritual self that is hidden within.

'Tis the human touch in this world that counts,
    The touch of your hand and mine,
Which means far more to the fainting heart
    Than shelter and bread and wine;
For shelter is gone when the night is o'er,
    And bread lasts only a day,
But the touch of the hand and the sound of the voice
    Sing on in the soul alway.

Spencer Michael Free

My Bouquet of Friendships

Just as we gather flowers
To make up a bright bouquet,
So do we gather friendships
As we go along life's way,
And as each different flower
Adds a charm that's all its own,
So each of our friendships brings a joy
That belongs to it alone.

Louise McClanahan

Friends Who Sail Together

There are friends who pass like ships in the night,
Who meet for a moment, then sail out of sight,
With never a backward glance of regret —
Friends we know briefly, then quickly forget...
There are other friends who sail together
Through quiet waters and stormy weather,
Helping each other through joy and through strife —
And they are the kind who give meaning to life!

Author Unknown

A MORNING THANKSGIVING

I awoke this morning with devout thanks-
giving for my friends, the old and the
new. Shall I not call God the Beautiful,
Who daily showeth Himself so to me in
His gifts? I chide society, I embrace solitude,
and yet I am not so ungrateful as not to see
the wise, the lovely, and the noble minded,
as from time to time they pass my gate.
Who hears me, who understands me, becomes
mine — a possession for all time. Nor is
Nature so poor but she gives me this joy
several times, and thus we weave social
threads of our own, a new web of relations;
and, as many thoughts in succession sub-

stantiate themselves, we shall by-and-by
stand in a new world of our own creation,
and no longer strangers and pilgrims in a
traditionary globe. My friends have come
to me unsought. The great God gave
them to me.

Ralph Waldo Emerson

We have been friends together
In sunshine and in shade.

Caroline Norton

I believe in God, in the same way in which I believe in my friends, because I feel the breath of His love and His invisible, intangible hand, bringing me here, carrying me there, pressing upon me.

Miguel de Unamuno

Solaces of Life

A garden bright with pink and gold,
Full harvest as the year grows old.

For every day some bookly gain;
For twilight, music's sweet refrain.

A dozen friends with gifts of cheer,
And love, more tender year by year.

With these, and Springtime at the door —
What mortal man could ask for more?

Thomas Curtis Clarke

Worthy of My Friends

If I could have but just one plea,
I think that that one prayer would be,
With all that such a prayer portends —
"Lord, make me worthy of my friends.

Help me to be the kind of man
That loyal friends believe I am.
Help me to be as true and fine
As they believe — these friends of mine.

Give me the courage under stress
That they expect me to possess;
And when they smile and look at me,
Oh, let me be, Lord, what they see!

Help me all pretense to forego,
And simply, without pomp or show,
Repay with true sincerity
The loyal faith they have in me.

And if, sometimes, I may have erred
In any thought or deed or word,
Then help me, Lord, to make amends —
Lord, make me worthy of my friends."

Helen Lowrie Marshall

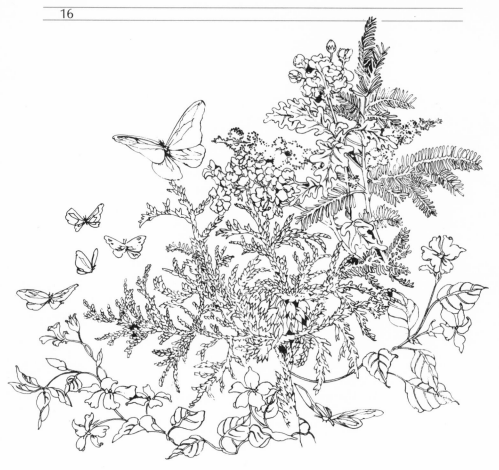

Speaking of Friendship

We were discussing it
a week ago,
how loosely it is used to signify
acquaintances or people passing by
and meaning little; how few really know
the depth of meaning in the countersign
we signal with so freely,
    "friend of mine."

There are a hundred vivid similes;
a fuller rapture when our joy is high;
when life is chill, a flame
    to warm us by;
in utter pain, remembered ecstasies....
Oh, words are weak! But you
    to whom I write
know what it is, alive
and rich and bright!

For once or twice within a lifetime, we
find someone whom we love
    for that which is
dependent not on looks or qualities...
call it soul, spirit, personality...
the thing which is no other but that one,
the thing which will not die
    when life is done.

And that we join to us in such a way
that neither fate nor change
    nor ill repute
can ever grow so strong as to refute
the bond, nor time bring any least decay....
Friendship like this, if life
    holds only one
it is well lived and heaven half begun.

Florence B. Jacobs

What I Live For

I live for those who love me,
    Whose hearts are kind and true;
For the Heaven that smiles above me,
    And awaits my spirit too;
For all human ties that bind me,
For the task by God assigned me,
For the bright hopes yet to find me,
    And the good that I can do.

G. Linnaeus Banks

You Have a Friend

Ye are my friends, if ye do whatsoever I command you.
Henceforth I call you not servants; for the servant knoweth
not what his lord doeth: but I have called you friends; for
all things that I have heard of my Father I have made known
unto you. Ye have not chosen me, but I have chosen you, and
ordained you, that ye should go and bring forth fruit, and
that your fruit should remain; that whatsoever ye shall ask
of the Father in my name, he may give it you.

John 15:14-16

Thank You, Friend

I never came to you, my friend,
And went away without
Some new enrichment of the heart:
More faith, and less of doubt,
More courage for the days ahead,
And often in great need
Coming to you, I went away
Comforted, indeed.

How can I find the shining words,
The glowing phrase that tells
All that your love has meant to me,
All that your friendship spells?
There is no word, no phrase for you
On whom I so depend,
All I can say to you is this:
God bless you, precious friend.

Grace Noll Crowell

Your Gift

You've given me a priceless gift
  I handle with great care,
The golden gift of friendship,
  So wonderful and fair.

Because of this, I'm wiser,
  And I think I'm kinder, too;
How many things in life I missed,
  Dear Friend, till I met you.

I never knew the glory
  That surrounds God's earth and skies
Until one day I learned to see
  True beauty through your eyes.

The gentleness that's part of you
  Is like the flowers that grow,
Making life more beautiful
  Through days that come and go.

You bring a warmth of deep content
  And understanding, too;
O Friend of mine, I didn't know
  What friendship was...till YOU!

Grace Easley

That best portion

of a good man's life...

His little, nameless,

unremembered acts

of kindness and of love.

William Wordsworth

Friend to Everyone

We follow Jesus in and out of homes; children cluster about His feet; women love Him; a dozen men leave net and plough to bind to His their fortunes, and others go forth by twos, not ones, to imitate Him. "Friend of publicans and sinners" was His title with those who loved Him not. Across the centuries we like and trust Him all the more because He was a man of many friends.

William C. Gannett

Song for Back Doors

Front doors are stately, proud and fine,
They let you in to call or dine,
Or if you ring at two or three,
They grant small talk and cakes and tea;
But back doors with their faded looks
Frame kittens, sunlight, boys and cooks,
They let you in without a bell
And friend to friend your secrets tell
While punctuating from a shelf
With apple pie, you serve yourself.
The front door is mind's counterpart,
The back door hinges on the heart.

Gladys McKee

Reflections

In a puddle by the roadside
Left by the warm, spring rain,
Its waters dark and muddy
With the brown earth stain,
I saw a glorious mountain
That stood up bold and high
Reflected in the water,
With a patch of cloud-decked sky.

Sometimes in folk around me
With burdens, hurts and fears:
Through joyful, happy hours
And often through their tears:
In some loving acts of kindness
As they show how much they care —
In the lives of folk around me
I find God reflected there.

Cyrus E. Albertson

Fireside Hour

There by the fire —
Soft candlelight —
Curtains drawn
Against the night.

Crackling firewood,
Amber tea —
Light talk flowing
Fast and free.

Nothing of false
Pretense or sham —
Just good friends sharing
Muffins and jam.

Katherine Edelman

Isn't It Fine

Isn't it fine, I say,
   A wealth of friends to gain,
Who share and bear, who love and smile
   The same through sun and rain.

Will Lauher

Friends Are Not a One-Way Street

Friendships can be infinitely varied.

And by their very differentness the whole pattern of one's days can be enlivened, and in so many ways rewarding.

Sift through your friendships; sort them.

There is the rich inner circle of those people who are dearest to the heart. Usually these are the persons to whom we can most honestly express our deepest selves. And even though we may not see them for days, weeks on end — even years — the bond remains strong and special and true.

Yet would we not be the poorer without the infinite variety of others?

Friends can be friends for so many different reasons.

There is the wonderfully helpful neighbor who is always willing to give you a hand with the children, or whip up a skirt for you.

There is the witty one who can always make you laugh.

There is the one who sends over bones for the dog, and is generous with praise for your growing crew.

There is the quiet soul who occasionally comes up with a startling gem of philosophy.

It takes patience sometimes to appreciate the true value in the people with whom circumstances have surrounded us. It takes awareness to recognize these values when they appear.

Yet almost everyone has something uniquely his own to contribute to our lives — and equally important, a place in his own life that perhaps we alone can satisfy.

The heart has many doors. Don't be too quick to bolt them.

Marjorie Holmes

Heavenly Bliss

He has the substance of all bliss
To whom a virtuous friend is given:
So sweet harmonious friendship is,
Add but eternity, you'll make it heaven.

John Norris

Borrowing

Someone has said, "If you want your friends to remember you, borrow something from them." I want to turn this around and say, if you want to remember your friends, be sure to borrow from them. Borrow faith, hope, and love. Borrow courage, humility, and integrity. Borrow their Christian example of the unseen values of the soul. Borrow their confidence in the living God and their loyalty to the triumphant Christ. Then indeed your days will be filled with strength.

John W. McKelvey

Father, Thank You

Father, thank you for the friend
Who brightens all my days —
The kind of friend who understands
My feelings and my ways.

Thank you for the friend who listens
When I have a need —
The friend who, when I fail,
Will make me feel that I succeed.

Father, thank you for the friend
Who's strong where I am weak —
Who doesn't criticize or scorn
The secret thoughts I speak.

Thank you for the friend who gives
Affection deep and true,
For, Father, that's the kind of friend
Who gives me part of You.

Richie Tankersley

Everyday Prayer

Let me be a little kinder, let me be a little blinder
To the faults of those about me; let me praise a little more.
Let me be, when I am weary, just a little bit more cheery.
Let me serve a little better those that I am striving for.
Let me be a little braver when temptation bids me waver.
Let me strive a little harder to be all that I should be.
Let me be a little meeker with the brother that is weaker.
Let me think more of my neighbor and a little less of me.

Author Unknown

Making This Life Worthwhile

May every soul that touches mine —
Be it the slightest contact —
Get therefrom some good;
Some little grace; one kindly thought;
One aspiration yet unfelt;
One bit of courage
For the darkening sky;
One gleam of faith
To brave the thickening ills of life;
One glimpse of brighter skies
Beyond the gathering mists —
To make this life worthwhile.

George Eliot

Your Friendship

Your friendship is the glowing sun...That warms the winding road...And lightens every step I take...Beneath my daily load...It is the soft and silvery note...That leaves the convent bell...The tender flower that I pick...To wear in my lapel...It is the murmur of the brook...The laughter of a child...And all the fragrance and romance...Of woods and grasses wild...Your friendship is the echo in...The hills that hold the dawn...And every dream that lingers when...The purple dusk is gone...It is the quiet gentleness...Of winds that walk the sea...It is the all-embracing gift...My God has given me.

James J. Metcalfe

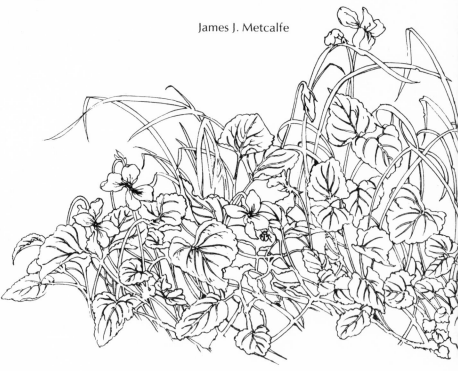

FRIENDSHIP is...

Finding no need

    to explain one's actions —

        feeling at ease and comfortable.

Idling away an evening

    in conversation — imitating

        one another's virtues.

Ending a visit

    with a warm handshake —

        enduring together.

Dividing our catch

    of fish — sharing our interests —

        maintaining our loyalty at all times.

Speaking our true sentiments —
   sharing our joys and our sorrows —
    staying out late together.
Having the ability to accept
   another's weaknesses — hearing
    a person out.
Initiating a surprise party —
   indicating our approvals —
    invoking our friend's approval.
Realizing one another's needs —
   recognizing one another's talents —
    restoring one another's faith.

Richard J. Marince

A "Glad" Friend

I have never liked gladioli. They have a stateliness that I have found forbidding, a restraint in their blooming that my unrestraint defied. Worst of all, they are too often found in bunches, fuchsias clashing with reds and oranges, like a group of beautiful women whose profusion has the effect of making beauty tiresome.

But at last I have made friends with one, a solitary glad in a crystal vase here on the kitchen table. As the Little Prince tamed his rose in St. Exupéry's profound book, I have "tamed" this glad. I spaded the earth and planted the bulb, drove away the hostile weeds, and carried water that she might flourish. I scoffed at myself knowing that this labor would not afford the joy that such diligence deserved. Then came the unexpected thrill of seeing her blooming among the green spires.

Now here in my kitchen I admire her, and her delicacy and restraint at last strike a responsive chord in me. So much of life is here on this stalk—birth and maturation, fruition and death. And thus this friend reveals herself gradually, like every other friend I've known. It is sad to think of the joy I should have missed had I never come to know this one gladiolus well.

Sad, to think that people, like glads, are all too often judged in "bunches" rather than on their individual merit as fruitful, blooming stalks.

Patricia Penton Leimback

Why God Gave Us Friends

God knew that everybody needs
Companionship and cheer.
He knew that people need someone
Whose thoughts are always near.
He knew they needed someone kind
To lend a helping hand,
Someone to gladly take the time
To care and understand...
    That's why God gave us friends....

He knew that we all need someone
To share each happy day,
To be a source of courage
When troubles come our way,
Someone to be true to us
Whether near or far apart,
Someone whose love we'll always hold
And treasure in our hearts...
    That's why God gave us friends.

Dean Walley

Beloved Memories

It has been said that life has treated me harshly; and sometimes I have complained in my heart because many pleasures
of human experience have been withheld from me, but when
I recollect the treasure of friendship that has been bestowed
upon me I withdraw all charges against life. If much has
been denied me, much, very much has been given me. So
long as the memory of certain beloved friends lives in my
heart I shall say that life is good.

Helen Keller

There is in friendship
something of all relations
and something above them all.
It is the golden thread
that ties the hearts of all the world.

John Evelyn

For Simple Things

No formal prayer is mine today,
But with an earnest heart which brings
To God its gratitude, I do
Give thanks for simple things.

The roof which shields me from the storm,
Where safe beneath a child's voice sings,
The task which needs my hands — I now
Give thanks for simple things.

The rose which blooms beside my door,
The crimson flash of cardinals' wings
That seek my old elm tree — yes, I
Give thanks for simple things.

The friend who understands, my bread
Each day — not wealth or power of kings
Does mean as much — how well I can
Give thanks for simple things!

Mary Hoge Bruce

God's Own Gift

Hearts are linked to hearts by God. The friend on whose
fidelity you can count, whose success in life flushes your
cheek with honest satisfaction, whose triumphant career
you have traced and read with a heart throbbing almost as
if it were a thing alive, for whose honour you would answer
as for your own; that friend, given to you by circumstances
over which you have no control, was God's own gift.

F. W. Robertson

Chain of Gold

Friendship is a chain of gold
Shaped in God's all-perfect mold;
Each link a smile, a laugh, a tear,
A touch of the hand, a word of cheer.

Author Unknown

Picture Puzzle

The puzzle in my idle hand releases
Its forms that fitted perfectly together.
This is my life, I think; these cardboard pieces
Good friends .... Friends are my spirit's golden weather,
Each in his place, contributing to me
His part in the long day's serenity,
And with the slightest missing one, my soul
Jarred from its promise of the pictured Whole.

Anne Campbell

A Friend

In the hour of distress and misery the eye of every mortal
turns to friendship; in the hour of gladness and conviviality,
what is our want? It is friendship. When the heart overflows
with gratitude, or with any other sweet and sacred sentiment,
what is the word to which it would give utterance? A friend.

Walter S. Landor

What Is a Friend?

What is a Friend? I'll tell you.
It is a person with whom you dare to be yourself.
Your soul can go naked with him.
He seems to ask you to put on nothing, only to be what
   you really are,
When you are with him, you do not have to be on your
   guard.
You can say what you think, so long as it is genuinely
   you.
He understands those contradictions in your nature that
   cause others to misjudge you.
With him you breathe freely — you can avow your little
   vanities and envies and absurdities and in opening them
   up to him they are dissolved on the white ocean of his
   loyalty.
He understands. — You can weep with him, laugh with him,
   pray with him — through and underneath it all he sees,
   knows and loves you.
A Friend — I repeat — is *one with whom you dare to be
   yourself.*

Author Unknown

If a man could mount to heaven
and survey the mighty universe,
his admiration of its beauties
would be much diminished
unless he had someone
to share in his pleasure.

Cicero

Men and Angels

Friendship, peculiar boon of heaven,
 The noble mind's delight and pride,
To men and angels only given,
 To all the lower world denied.

Samuel Johnson

No Greater Blessing

There is no greater blessing
Than an understanding friend
Who's there in times of trouble
And on whom we can depend,
A friend who knows our every mood
And brightens cloudy days,
One who's slow to criticize
But quick to offer praise....

There is no greater blessing
Than a friend who always cares,
One who will remember us
In daily thoughts and prayers,
One who shares our happy times
And gives them added worth,
Who adds a touch of heaven
To all our days on earth.

Kay Andrew

THE ART OF FRIENDSHIP

A friend is "like the shadow of a great
rock in a weary land," a source
of refuge and strength to those who
walk in darkness.

A friend strives to lift people up, not
cast them down; to encourage, not
discourage.

A friend is sensitively responsive to
the dreams and aims of others and
shows sincere appreciation for the
contributions others make to the
enrichment of life.

A friend is himself, he is done with
hypocrisy, artificiality and pretense,
he meets and mingles with people
in quiet simplicity and humility.

A friend is tolerant, he has an understanding heart and a forgiving
nature.

Wilferd A. Peterson

Ah, how good it feels –
the hand of an old friend.

Henry Wadsworth Longfellow

Down Life's Highway

Hand in hand, together,
    Traveling life's highway;
We find the journey pleasant,
    Sharing day by day.

Sharing the sweet and the bitter,
    Sharing the pleasure and pain;
We take the sun with the shadow,
    Laugh at the silver rain.

Laugh at the storms and brave them,
    Seeking to understand;
We find the fruit of life sweeter
    Traveling hand in hand.

Emily Carey Alleman

Part of God's Plan

What made us friends in the long ago
When first we met?
Well I think I know;
The best in me and the best in you
Hailed each other because they knew
That always and always since life began
Our being friends was part of God's plan.

Author Unknown

If instead of a gem, or even a flower,
we should cast the gift of a loving thought
into the heart of a friend,
that would be giving
as the angels give.

George MacDonald

Influence

Drop a pebble in the water,
And its ripples reach out far;
And the sunbeams dancing on them
May reflect them to a star.

Give a smile to someone passing,
Thereby making his morning glad;
It may greet you in the evening
When your own heart may be sad.

Do a deed of simple kindness;
Though its end you may not see,
It may reach, like widening ripples,
Down a long eternity.

Joseph Norris

We cannot tell the precise moment when friendship is formed. As in filling a vessel drop by drop, there is at last a drop which makes it run over. So in a series of kindnesses... there is at last one which makes the heart run over.

James Boswell

The Country of Friendship

When God was finished with land and sea,
River and stream, with fruit and tree,
With dark and light, shadow and sun,
With Adam and Eve, He added one
More rare delight to warm the heart,
Beyond all kin; I see Him start
The shape, the pattern, happy blend
Of caring and sharing...God made a friend.

Gladys McKee

If trust is the first requisite
for making a friend,
faithfulness is the first requisite
for keeping him.

Hugo Black

Special People

People who know
how to brighten a day
with heartwarming smiles
and with kind words they say,
People who know
how to gently impart
the comfort it takes
to cheer somebody's heart,
People who know
how to always come through
when there's anything
they can possibly do,
People who know
how to willingly share,
who know how to give
and who know how to care,
who know how to let
all their warm feelings show
are people that others
feel lucky to know.

Karen Ravn

Keeping in Touch

What's better than the telephone
(Especially when we're alone)
To brighten up a nothing day,
To chase the Monday blues away,
To let us know a friend is there
Who says "I'm glad."…"I'll help."…"I care."…
The telephone brings others near,
Brings joy and laughter, warmth and cheer.
How many times our hearts rejoice
To hear a dear, familiar voice!
What better way is there to spend
Pleasured moments friend to friend?

Katherine Nelson Davis

THE PARABLE OF THE GOOD SAMARITAN

A certain man was going down from Jerusalem to Jerico, when robbers attacked him, stripped him and beat him up, leaving him half dead. It so happened that a priest was going down that road; when he saw the man he walked on by, on the other side. In the same way a Levite came there, went over and looked at the man, and then walked on by, on the other side. But a certain Samaritan who was traveling that way came upon him, and when he saw the man his heart was filled with pity. He went over to him, poured oil and wine on his wounds and bandaged them; then he put the man on his own animal and took him to an inn, where he took care of him. The next day he took out two silver coins and gave them to the innkeeper. "Take care of him," he told the innkeeper, "and when I come back this way I will pay you back whatever you spend on him." And Jesus concluded, "Which one of these three seems to you to have been a neighbor to the man attacked by the robbers?"

from the Gospel of Luke

To Friendship

A friend is someone lovely who
Cuts her chrysanthemums for you
And, giving, cares not for the cost,
Nor sees the blossoms she has lost;
But rather, values friendship's store,
Gives you her best and grows some more.

Eleanor Long

Heart's Treasure

The toys and blocks with which we play
Are houses, lands, and gold.
Their values quickly pass away,
As does a tale that's told.

But kindly, gracious deeds abide,
Their wealth will not depart;
Their flowers of joy are multiplied
In gardens of the heart.

Charles Russell Wakeley

Thank Heaven for Friends

Life isn't much fun
Or as pleasurable, is it,
Unless we have friends
To come over and visit,
Or without a good neighbor
From whom we can borrow,
Or someone to say,
"Let's go shopping tomorrow!"
And wouldn't we miss
At our garage sale each spring
A friend to help price
And sell everything?
Our lives would be dreary
Without someone near us
To share in our dreams,
To encourage and cheer us;
If we had no rapport
With others, we'd be
Missing such joy,
Such camaraderie!
So — thank heaven for friends —
They help us survive,
And add to the pleasure
Of being alive!

Katherine Nelson Davis

Comparisons

Friendship — Like music heard on the waters,
Like pines when the wind passeth by,
Like pearls in the depths of the ocean,
Like stars that enamel the sky,
Like June and the odor of roses,
Like dew and the freshness of morn,
Like sunshine that kisseth the clover,
Like tassels of silk on the corn,
Like mountains that arch the blue heavens,
Like clouds when the sun dippeth low,
Like songs of birds in the forest,
Like brooks where the sweet waters flow,
Like dreams of Arcadian pleasures,
Like colors that gratefully blend,
Like everything breathing of kindness —
Like these is the love of a friend.

A. P. Stanley

Set in Optima.
Printed on Hallmark Eggshell Book paper.
Book design and calligraphy by Rick Cusick.
The designer gratefully acknowledges
the assistance of Rainer Koenig.